G000295634

Made with love

By

....

Introduction

Dear mum this journal created as a memory book for your unique life story. It is time for you to write and cherish your own life story and it always needs to be remembered & treasured.

The pages are guided with prompts so you can have all those moments written down for your grandchild to recall and look back on and read later the book will become a treasured family keepsake.

The plain pages can be used for writing in as well as sticking in photos and other mementos for a special occasion.

Then have fun filling this book and give to your Grandchild

CHILDHOOD

Can you tell me about the time and place you were born?

What are your earliest memories growing up?

Where did you live as a child?

What do you remember of your childhood home?

Tell me about your family?
What are your parent's names?

What do you remember most about your Mom and Dad?

What are your best memories with
your grandparents?

What interesting stories do you know
about other people in your family?

What were your favourite
childhood toys or games?

Did you have a pet growing up?
What were their names?

Did you have holidays as a child and
what do you remember about them?

Tell me about your friends when you were a child.
Who was your best friend?

Can you share some unforgettable memories of your school life? and who was your favourite teacher? why?

Tell me an interesting or funny
story about your childhood?

What did you want to be when you grew up?

Tell me about any books you liked to read or films or TV shows you used to watch?

ADULTHOOD

How do you remember your
teenage years?

What music did you listen to and what films do you remember as a teenage?

Did you ever have your heart broken?

What was your first job? How much
money did you make?

What do you wish you had done then that
you didn't do?

Did you still have the same childhood friends growing up?

Did you make new friends as a young
adult ?

What have you always wanted? Did you ever get it?

What's the best place you've traveled?

Have you won any special awards or prizes as an adult? What were they for?

What has been your favourite saying
or quote?

Do you have any regrets?
Why or Why not?

How did you meet Dad
How did you get engaged?

Where was your wedding? Tell me about your wedding ceremony?

What's your favorite thing about your partner

MOTHERHOOD

strong

AS A

Mom

What do you think about being a parent?

What was your biggest fear about having children?

What's the best thing about being a mother?

What do you remember about when each
of us was born?

Were there any similarities between me
and you as a child?

What do you want your children and grandchildren to remember about you?

What was the most rewarding thing about
raising kids?

When were you proudest of me?

What's your favorite memory of us?

What's a time that you felt worried or afraid for me?

What do you want your children and grandchildren to remember about you?

What are you most thankful for?

What are you most proud of in life?

What did you find most beautiful about life?

Can you name a few of your favourite things?

What advise were you given by your parents?

What advise would you give me?

What was the best day in your life so far?

What are some values you hold?

What's the most trouble you've ever gotten in?

What is your most embarrassing moment?

What was a historic moment that you lived through?
Can you tell me about it?

Is there anything left on your bucket list?

Home is where my Mum Is

he rest the book is for any stories that you may want to tell
and memories that you would like to share.
You can also doodle or sketch anything that you feel is adding to your story

Printed in Great Britain
by Amazon